## Jill Dupleix

# Malaysian

# JILL DUPLEIX

# Malaysian

*Photography by Simon Wheeler*

WEIDENFELD & NICOLSON

# Jill Dupleix

Jill Dupleix is one of Australia's most inspirational food writers, with a passion for all things hot and spicy. She is the author of eight cook books, including *hot food cool jazz*, a best-selling collection of Malaysian hawker stall recipes accompanied by a CD of modern jazz. She is also the food editor of *The Sydney Morning Herald* and *Elle Australia*, and is a popular food commentator on radio and television.

Jill lives in Sydney, Australia, and frequently travels throughout Asia to visit the fresh food markets and collect recipes. She is perfectly placed to translate the mysteries of the Orient into fast and fabulous meals for the home kitchen.

# Contents

# If you like good food,
# cook it yourself.

LI LIWENG
*(17th century)*

# Introduction

Malaysian food is easy to love. It has the fire of chilli, the scent of spices, the lushness of wild leaves, the creaminess of coconut, the slinkiness of noodles, the steam of soup, the smoky breath of the *kuali* (wok), the sweetness of palm sugar, the tang of lime and the sourness of tamarind, calling all the senses into play.

One mouthful of fast and fiery blachan spinach, smoky fried rice noodles, spicy chilli-fried squid, or sweet sago pudding is all it takes to light the fire of your own personal passion for this earthy, sensual, satisfying cuisine.

In this collection, I have pinched recipes from my favourite hawker stalls in Singapore and Kuala Lumpur, from the great women cooks of the Nonya tradition, and from Malaysian friends and families everywhere.

You don't need special equipment, nor a pantry of unpronounceable ingredients. Just a few spices, some garlic, ginger and shallots, and a spirit of kitchen adventure. And remember, all Malaysian food tastes better accompanied by lots of laughter, music and friends.

*Jill Dupleix*

# LOH BAK
## *Deep-fried pork and prawn rolls*

**MAKES 10**

200 g/7 oz uncooked prawns in
their shells
250 g/9 oz minced pork
2 tablespoons grated carrot
6 water chestnuts, finely
chopped
1 tablespoon finely chopped
fresh coriander
2 spring onions, finely chopped
½ teaspoon five-spice powder
½ teaspoon salt
1 tablespoon light soy sauce
1 egg, lightly beaten
1 pack (100 g/3½ oz) large dried
beancurd skins (page 34)
1 teaspoon cornflour blended
with 1 tablespoon cold water
vegetable oil for deep-frying

**To serve**
sweet chilli sauce

Devein the prawns by hooking out the intestinal tract
with a thin bamboo skewer. Shell and chop to a fine
paste. Mix the prawns, pork, carrot, water chestnuts,
coriander, spring onions, five-spice powder, salt,
soy sauce and egg in a bowl and leave to stand for
10 minutes.

Cut the beancurd skins into ten 15 cm/6 inch squares
and wipe with a clean, damp cloth to soften them. Put 2
tablespoons of the prawn mixture in the centre of each
square and brush the edges with the cornflour mixture.
Roll up tightly from one corner to the opposite corner,
tucking in the sides to form a spring roll shape.

Heat the oil to 180–190°C/350–375°F or until a cube
of bread browns in 30 seconds. Deep-fry two rolls at a
time for 3–4 minutes, turning once, until golden. Slice
each roll on the diagonal into two or three pieces, and
pile on to a serving plate. Serve with small dipping
bowls of sweet chilli sauce.

*Serve as an appetizer with drinks, or as a first course. Follow
with beef rendang (page 22) and roti jala (page 26), and finish
with sago pudding (page 32).*

# SATAY AYAM
## Chicken satay

**SERVES 8 AS A STARTER,
4 AS A MAIN COURSE**

500 g/1 lb 2 oz chicken
  thigh meat
6 shallots or 1 onion, finely
  chopped
1 garlic clove, crushed
1 tablespoon grated fresh ginger
1 stalk of lemongrass, peeled
  and sliced
1 tablespoon brown sugar or
  palm sugar
½ teaspoon salt
1 teaspoon turmeric
1 teaspoon ground cumin
1 teaspoon ground coriander
200 ml/7 fl oz coconut milk

**To serve**
Peanut sauce (page 37) or
  sweet chilli sauce

Soak 20–24 bamboo skewers in cold water for 4–5 hours to prevent them from burning.

Cut the chicken into thin strips about 5 cm/2 inches long and 2 cm/¾ inch wide.

Grind, pound or blend the shallots or onion, garlic, ginger and lemongrass together, then add the sugar, salt, turmeric, cumin, coriander and coconut milk and mix until smooth. Marinate the chicken pieces in the coconut mixture for at least 2 hours or overnight.

Thread two or three strips of meat on to each bamboo skewer, being sure to cover the pointed end. Heat a lightly oiled grill until very hot: satay is at its best cooked outside over a bed of glowing charcoal, the coals fanned to create even more smoke to flavour the meat.

Grill the satay on both sides until golden, brushing with the marinade while grilling. Serve hot, with peanut sauce or sweet chilli sauce for dipping.

*Serve as an appetizer or a main course, accompanied by plates of chilled cucumber and steamed rice. Finish the meal with fresh, ripe mangoes or a refreshing mango and yoghurt lassi.*

# OTAK OTAK
## Grilled fish in banana leaf

**MAKES 12**

500 g/1 lb 2 oz fish fillet
3 dried red chillies, soaked and
  drained (page 34)
5 candlenuts or macadamia nuts
1 onion, grated
1 tablespoon blachan (dried
  shrimp paste)
1 teaspoon turmeric
1 egg, beaten
2 tablespoons coconut milk
1 tablespoon palm sugar or white
  sugar
1 teaspoon salt
4 banana leaves or 12 dried
  lotus leaves, soaked until
  pliable

Using a fork, scrape the fish into fine flakes and place in a bowl, or briefly blend to a paste in a food processor. Add 4 tablespoons water, a tablespoon at a time, beating with a wooden spoon until it feels light and fluffy.

Pound or grind the drained chillies, nuts, onion, blachan and turmeric together to make a paste. Mix the paste with the fish, then add the egg and beat well. Add the coconut milk, sugar and salt.

Cut the banana leaves into 15 cm/6 inch squares and dip into boiling water for 2 minutes to soften them. Drain and pat dry. Place 2 tablespoons of the fish mixture in the centre of each square and roll up to form open-ended tubes. Fasten each end with a strong cocktail stick.

Heat the grill until very hot. Brush the banana leaves lightly with oil and grill for about 5 minutes on each side, until the leaves are slightly charred and the filling is firm when pressed.

*Serve as an appetizer followed by a Malaysian curry, or as part of a shared meal with coconut rice (page 37), curries and sambals. Finish with thin crepes (kueh dadar) with a sweet coconut filling.*

# SAMBAL SOTONG
## Chilli-fried squid

**SERVES 4**

500 g/1 lb 2 oz small squid
  (sotong)
2 tablespoons tamarind pulp
1 stalk of lemongrass, peeled
  and sliced
1 garlic clove, crushed
4 dried red chillies, soaked and
  drained (page 34)
1 teaspoon blachan (dried
  shrimp paste)
1 onion, chopped
2 tablespoons peanut oil
½ teaspoon salt
2 teaspoons palm sugar or
  brown sugar

Clean the squid using the method on page 36. Cut the tubes lengthwise and use the tip of the knife to lightly score a crisscross pattern on the surface, without cutting right through. Cut into 5 cm/2 inch squares and set aside, with the tentacles.

Soak the tamarind pulp in 125 ml/4 fl oz boiling water and leave for 5 minutes. Knead to dissolve, then strain the tamarind water and set aside.

Grind, pound or blend the lemongrass, garlic, drained chillies, blachan and onion together to make a paste.

Heat a wok until hot, then add the oil. When the oil is hot, add the chilli paste and stir-fry for 2 minutes. Add the tamarind water, salt and sugar and stir-fry for 3 minutes. Add the squid meat and tentacles and stir-fry over high heat for 3−4 minutes, until cooked but still tender.

*Serve this spicy, substantial sambal with a bowl of steamed rice and a platter of stir-fried green beans, as part of a shared Malaysian meal. Follow with a sticky rice dessert drizzled with coconut milk and palm sugar.*

# CILI UDANG
## Chilli prawns

**SERVES 4–6**

1 kg/2¼ lb uncooked prawns in
  their shells
3 tablespoons vegetable oil
2 garlic cloves, crushed
2 slices of fresh ginger
4 dried red chillies, soaked,
  drained and chopped
  (page 34)
3 tablespoons chilli sauce, or to
  taste
125 ml/4 fl oz tomato sauce or
  ketchup
375 ml/12 fl oz hot chicken
  stock
½ teaspoon salt
2 teaspoons sugar, or to taste
2 teaspoons cornflour blended
  with 2 tablespoons cold water
4 spring onions, chopped
2 small eggs, beaten
fresh coriander leaves

Devein the prawns by hooking out the intestinal tract
with a thin bamboo skewer.

Heat the oil in a wok and fry the prawns quickly over
high heat until almost cooked. Drain and set aside.

Drain off all but 1 tablespoon of the oil and reheat the
wok. Add the garlic and ginger and cook for 3 minutes.
Add the chopped chillies, chilli sauce, tomato sauce,
stock, salt and sugar, and stir well to mix. Add the cornflour paste, bring to the boil, stirring constantly, and stir
for 1 minute.

Return the prawns to the wok, together with the spring
onions, and toss to coat. Slowly drizzle in the eggs,
stirring all the time. Cook for a further 1–2 minutes,
until you have a creamy, thick sauce. Serve immediately,
scattered with coriander leaves.

*Serve with plenty of coconut rice (page 37) or steamed jasmine
rice to soak up the juices. Start the meal with chicken satay
and peanut sauce (page 12) and finish with banana fritters
(goreng pisang).*

# CHAR KUEH TEOW
## Fried rice noodles with pork and prawns

**SERVES 4–6**

500 g/1 lb 2 oz fresh rice
noodles (kueh teow)
125 g/4 oz fresh beansprouts
200 g/7 oz fresh squid tubes,
cleaned (page 36)
2 tablespoons peanut oil
2 garlic cloves, crushed
3 dried red chillies, soaked,
drained and pounded
(page 34)
200 g/7 oz barbecued roast
pork, finely sliced (char sieu),
or leftover roast pork,
or 2 Chinese sausages (lup
cheong), finely sliced on the
diagonal
12 small prawns, deveined and
shelled
1 tablespoon dark or mushroom
soy sauce
2 tablespoons light soy sauce
2 tablespoons oyster sauce
salt and pepper
2 eggs, lightly beaten
2 tablespoons finely chopped
spring onions (green parts)

Cut the noodles into 2 cm/¾ inch wide strips and place in a heatproof bowl. Pour boiling water on top and gently pull the noodles apart with chopsticks. Drain and rinse in cold water. Put the beansprouts in another bowl, pour boiling water over them, then drain and rinse in cold water.

Cut the squid tubes lengthwise and use the tip of the knife to lightly score a crisscross pattern on the surface, without cutting right through. Cut into 5 cm/2 inch squares.

Heat a wok until hot, then add the oil. When the oil is hot, add the garlic and fry for 1 minute, stirring. Add the pounded chillies and fry for 1 minute, stirring. Add the pork, prawns and squid and stir-fry over high heat for 2 minutes. Add dark and light soy sauces, oyster sauce, salt, pepper and beansprouts and stir-fry for 2 minutes. Add the noodles and cook over high heat for 3 minutes, tossing to coat the noodles in the sauce.

Make a well in the centre of the noodles and pour in the beaten eggs. Stir the eggs as they start to scramble, then cover with noodles and toss to combine. Add the spring onions and serve immediately.

*Serve as a shared main course, with some steamed tofu (beancurd) in peanut sauce (page 37), and finish with pulut hitam, a sweet black rice dessert.*

# RENDANG DAGING
## Beef and coconut curry

**SERVES 4–6**

3 tablespoons desiccated
  coconut
2 garlic cloves, crushed
6 shallots or 1 onion, sliced
2 stalks of lemongrass, peeled
  and sliced
6 dried red chillies, soaked and
  drained (page 34)
2 tablespoons grated fresh
  ginger
1 teaspoon turmeric
1 teaspoon salt
1 teaspoon sugar
2 tablespoons vegetable oil
600 g/1¼ lb topside of beef, cut
  into bite-sized cubes
250 ml/8 fl oz thick coconut milk
1 teaspoon tamarind pulp
  dissolved in 1 tablespoon
  water (page 35)
4 star anise
1 cinnamon stick

Heat a dry frying pan, add the coconut and toast until lightly golden. Pound or blend the toasted coconut, garlic, shallots or onion, lemongrass, drained chillies, ginger, turmeric, salt and sugar together to make a paste.

Heat the oil in a heavy-bottomed frying pan. Add the chilli paste and cook for 5 minutes, stirring, until fragrant. Add the beef and stir-fry for 5 minutes, until it changes colour.

Add the coconut milk, 125 ml/4 fl oz water, tamarind water, star anise and cinnamon stick and bring to the boil, stirring constantly.

Reduce the heat and simmer gently, uncovered, for 1½ hours, until the sauce has almost cooked away, and the beef is dark and tender. If it gets too dry while it is cooking, add a little water, but the sauce should only just coat the meat.

*Start the meal with drinks and crunchy little ikan bilis (tiny fried fish). Serve beef rendang with steamed rice, roti jala (page 26) and a spicy spinach sambal (page 28). Finish with coconut or pineapple ice cream.*

# Ikan gulai
## Fish curry with coconut milk

**SERVES 4**

500 g/1 lb 2 oz firm fish steaks
  e.g. cod, snapper
1½ tablespoons tamarind pulp
1 stalk of lemongrass, peeled
  and sliced
4 dried red chillies, soaked and
  drained (page 34)
1 tablespoon freshly grated
  ginger
2 garlic cloves, crushed
8 shallots or 1 onion, chopped
2 tablespoons vegetable oil
1 tablespoon ground coriander
1 teaspoon ground cumin
1 teaspoon ground fennel
1 teaspoon turmeric
6 curry leaves
1 teaspoon salt
1 teaspoon sugar
250 ml (8 fl oz) coconut milk

Remove any skin or bones from the fish and cut into bite-sized pieces.

Soak the tamarind pulp in 125 ml/4 fl oz boiling water and leave for 10 minutes. Knead to dissolve, then strain the tamarind water and set aside.

Grind, pound or blend the lemongrass, drained chillies, ginger, garlic and shallots together to make a paste.

Heat the oil in a wok or frying pan and fry the chilli paste for 5 minutes, stirring, until fragrant. Add the coriander, cumin, fennel, turmeric, curry leaves, salt and sugar, then slowly add the coconut milk, stirring. Bring to the boil, stirring constantly. Add the tamarind water and simmer, uncovered, for 10 minutes, until the sauce thickens slightly.

To serve, add the fish and simmer for 3–4 minutes, until just cooked.

*Start with a spicy chicken soup or spring rolls. Serve fish curry with plenty of rice and a stir-fried green vegetable such as green beans or water spinach (page 35).*

# ROTI JALA
## Lacy pancakes

**MAKES 6**

125 g/4 oz plain flour
½ teaspoon salt
250 ml/8 fl oz fresh milk or thin
  coconut milk
1 egg, well beaten
1 teaspoon vegetable oil, plus
  2 tablespoons for frying

Sift the flour and salt together into a bowl. Add the milk, egg and 1 teaspoon of the oil, and beat well until smooth. Leave to stand for 5 minutes.

Heat a heavy nonstick frying pan or wok, and brush lightly with oil. Drizzle thin lines of batter on to the hot pan in overlapping circles through a thin-holed sieve – you can pierce four small holes in an empty can, use a tomato sauce dispenser, or partially block off the tip of a funnel with your finger – to form a lacy pancake.

When the pancake is set on top and curling at the edges, turn and cook for 30 seconds on the other side, without letting it brown. Remove and fold into quarters. Oil the pan lightly between each pancake.

*Dip lacy pancakes into chicken, fish or beef curry, or stuff with minced meat or chicken. Or just sprinkle with sugar and eat at the end of a meal with cups of fragrant Chinese tea.*

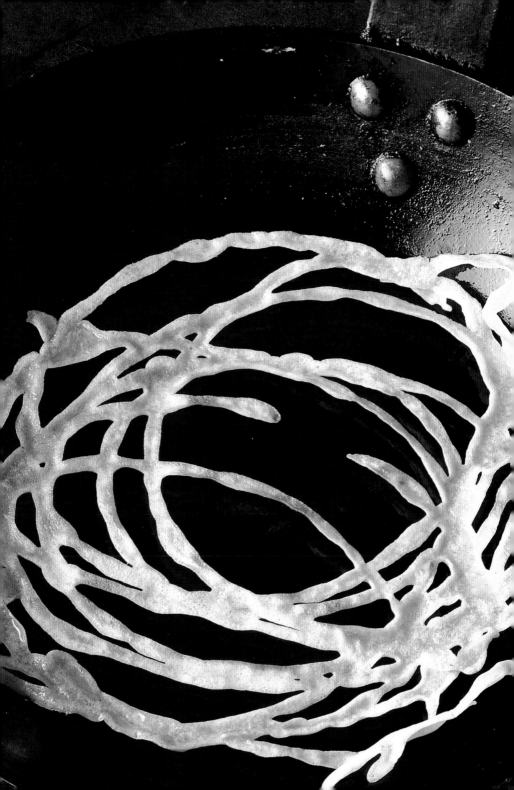

# BLACHAN KANG KONG
## Chilli-fried spinach

**SERVES 4**

500 g/1 lb 2 oz fresh water
  spinach (page 35) or regular
  spinach
2 dried red chillies, soaked and
  drained (page 34)
2 garlic cloves, crushed
2 candlenuts or macadamia nuts
6 shallots or 1 small onion,
  chopped
2 teaspoons blachan (dried
  shrimp paste)
1 tablespoon dried shrimps,
  ground
1 tablespoon vegetable oil
½ teaspoon salt
½ teaspoon sugar

Wash the spinach and shake dry.

Grind, pound or blend the drained chillies, garlic, nuts, shallots or onion, blachan and dried shrimps together to make a paste.

Heat the oil in a wok or frying pan and fry the paste for about 5 minutes, stirring, until fragrant. Add the spinach and toss to coat in the paste. As soon as the leaves start to wilt, add the salt and sugar, and keep tossing until the stems soften and leaves have wilted.

*Serve as a side dish to a fiery Malaysian curry, seafood sambal or fried noodles. Follow with a tropical fruit salad drizzled with coconut milk and palm sugar syrup.*

# MEE GORENG
## *Hokkien noodles with potato and tomato*

**SERVES 4**

2 squares of dried beancurd
  cake (page 34) or 4–6 pieces
  of fried beancurd
2 cooked potatoes
2 firm tomatoes
500 g/1 lb 2 oz fresh egg
  noodles
2 tablespoons vegetable oil
3 garlic cloves, pounded
1 onion, chopped
125 g/4 oz fresh beansprouts
2 tablespoons tomato sauce
  or ketchup
1 tablespoon chilli sauce,
  or to taste
2 tablespoons light soy sauce
½ teaspoon salt
½ teaspoon sugar
10 small uncooked prawns or
  shrimps, shelled
1 egg, beaten
2 spring onions, sliced

**To garnish**
2 tablespoons crisply fried
  shallots
½ small iceberg lettuce, finely
  shredded
1 lime or lemon, quartered

Cut the beancurd, potatoes and tomatoes into 1 cm/ ½ inch cubes; leave the tomatoes to drain. Pour boiling water over the noodles, then drain and rinse.

Heat a wok until hot, then add the oil. When the oil is hot, add the garlic and onion and fry until the onion is soft. Add the drained noodles and stir-fry for 2 minutes over high heat.

Add the beansprouts, potatoes, tomatoes, beancurd, tomato sauce, chilli sauce, soy sauce, salt, sugar and prawns and stir-fry over high heat until the prawns are cooked.

Tilt the wok, push the noodles to one side, and pour in the egg. Cover the egg with noodles and leave to set for 30 seconds over medium heat, then toss well. Add the spring onions, and serve topped with fried shallots, shredded lettuce and lime quarters.

*Start the meal with rojak, a Malaysian fruit and vegetable salad, and finish with ice kachang, a refreshing dessert of shaved ice and sweet things, such as sweetcorn kernels, peanuts and red azuki beans with palm sugar syrup and evaporated milk.*

# GULA MELAKA
## Sago pudding with palm sugar and coconut milk

**SERVES 6**

100 g/3½ oz palm sugar
  (page 35)
1 cup (250 ml/8 fl oz) pearl
  (small seed) sago
125 ml/4 fl oz thick coconut milk
pinch of salt

Put the palm sugar in a small saucepan with 250 ml/ 8 fl oz water and place over medium heat, stirring until the sugar has dissolved. Simmer until the liquid reduces to around 175 ml/6 fl oz. Leave to cool.

Bring 1.5 litres/2½ pints water to the boil in a saucepan. When it bubbles, add the sago in a slow, steady stream, stirring constantly. Cook, stirring, for 10–15 minutes, until the sago is soft and transparent. Drain and rinse under cold running water to wash off excess starch. Drain well.

Mix the sago with half the palm sugar syrup, half the coconut milk and the salt, and ladle into six 125 ml/ 4 fl oz moulds. Cover and chill for at least 1–2 hours.

To serve, unmould the chilled sago on to individual serving plates, and top each one with a spoonful of the remaining palm sugar syrup and a spoonful of chilled coconut milk.

*Serve on its own, or surrounded by fresh tropical fruits: mango, starfruit, papaya, pineapple. This pudding also goes well with a small espresso coffee!*

# The Basics

## GLOSSARY OF MALAYSIAN INGREDIENTS

**BANANA LEAVES**

Long green leaves used to wrap food before steaming, frying or grilling, or as a plate decoration. Dip into boiling water for 2 minutes to soften if using for wrapping.

**BARBECUED ROAST PORK**
*(CHAR SIEU)*

Available from Chinese roast meat specialists.

**BEANCURD CAKE, DRIED**
*(TAU KWA)*

Bought in squares from Asian food stores.

**BEANCURD SKINS, DRIED**
*(TAU FU JUK)*

The skin that forms on heated soybean milk is dried on bamboo mats to form soft, translucent sheets, sold fresh or frozen in Asian food stores. Use for wrapping foods before steaming or frying.

**BLACHAN**

Dried shrimp paste with a pungent smell; when cooked it gives a distinctive aromatic tang. To use, either toast or grind and fry with onions. Available in butter-like blocks, it should be stored in a screw-topped jar.

**CANDLENUTS**
*(BUAH KERAS)*

Used to thicken sauces and add creaminess and a nutty flavour. If unobtainable, substitute macadamia nuts.

**CHILLIES, DRIED RED**
*(CILI KERING)*

Soak in water for a few hours, then blend or pound with a little of the soaking water to make a reddish paste. If unobtainable, substitute fresh red chillies.

**CURRY LEAVES**
*(DAUN KARI)*

Small dark green leaves, available fresh or dried, often used in fish curries.

**FIVE-SPICE POWDER**

A popular Chinese seasoning made of ground star anise, fennel, cloves, cinnamon and Sichuan pepper.

| | |
|---|---|
| LEMONGRASS<br>(*SERAI*) | A fresh, tough reed grass with a strong lemon fragrance. Peel back to use only the tender white stalk. Slice and pound before use. |
| NOODLES, FRESH RICE<br>(*KUEH TEOW*) | Flat, glossy white noodles known as *pho* in Vietnam, *kueh teow* in Malaysia and *hor fun* in China. Available from Chinese food stores, cut or uncut. |
| NOODLES, HOKKIEN | Round yellow egg noodles available fresh from Asian food stores. If unobtainable, substitute dried egg noodles. |
| PALM SUGAR<br>(*GULA MELAKA*) | Brownish-black rolls of tree sap, sold in some Asian food stores. Break off a piece and dissolve in a little water, with a pandan leaf if you have one. Simmer until the sugar has melted, then strain. If unobtainable, substitute brown sugar with a touch of golden syrup. |
| PANDAN LEAF | Long, thin leaves used to add a fresh, lightly floral flavour to sugar syrups, custards and desserts. |
| SHRIMPS, DRIED<br>(*UDANG KERING*) | Should be a bright orange-pink. Soak in a little hot water for 10 minutes before cooking. Drain and toss into noodle dishes, stir-fries and rice. |
| STAR ANISE | Star-shaped spice with a haunting aniseed flavour. |
| TAMARIND<br>(*ASSAM JAWA*) | Tamarind pulp is the pressed pods of the tamarind tree. To make tamarind water, soak the required amount in a little boiling water for 5 minutes, then squeeze until dissolved, and strain. Add to a chicken soup or fish curry for a tongue-curling lemon-lime sourness. |
| WATER SPINACH<br>(*KANG KONG*) | A spinach-like green with hollow stems (*ong choy* in Chinese). Popular in soups and sambals. |

TO POUND TO A PASTE

Most Malaysian dishes start with a *rempah*, a paste pounded in a mortar with a pestle. You can blend the ingredients in a food processor but you won't get the authentic texture. When pounding, add tougher ingredients first (e.g. lemongrass stalk), then wet ingredients (e.g. onion), and get a good rhythm going.

TO GRIND SPICES

Freshly ground spices are the motherlode of Malaysian cooking. Where possible, start with the fresh whole spice, and lightly toast it in a hot, dry pan until fragrant. Grind to a powder, either in a mortar, or in a small electric coffee grinder reserved for spices.

TO CLEAN SQUID

Gently grasp the head and twist it out of the body. Pull out the inner bone. Cut off the tentacles just above the eyes, and squeeze and discard the small sphere that pops out. Discard all but the body tube and tentacles. Peel the skin from the tubes, rinse and pat dry.

TO MAKE FRESH
COCONUT MILK

Hold a fresh, heavy coconut in one hand over a bowl, and hit it with a hammer on its circumference, turning the coconut in your hand, until it cracks in half. Drain out the juice (chill and drink later), and grate the flesh on a coconut grater, or break into smaller, flatter pieces and use a normal grater (hard work).

Add enough hot water to cover the coconut flesh, and leave to soak for 10 minutes. When the water has cooled, squeeze the flesh through a strainer into a second bowl. Leave to stand for 30 minutes.

The coconut cream will rise to the top, leaving thin coconut milk below. Add a little salt, keep refrigerated and use the same day.

# Sambal satay (*Peanut sauce*)

**MAKES 300–450 ML/½–¾ PINT**

1 tablespoon tamarind pulp
  (page 35)
200 g/7 oz roasted peanuts
4 dried red chillies, soaked
  and drained (page 34)
4 shallots, roughly chopped
2 garlic cloves, crushed
4 candlenuts or macadamia
  nuts
1 stalk of lemongrass, peeled
  and sliced
2 tablespoons vegetable oil
250 ml/8 fl oz coconut milk
2 tablespoons palm or brown
  sugar
1 teaspoon salt

Soak the tamarind in 2 tablespoons boiling water for 10 minutes, then squeeze and knead until dissolved. Strain the tamarind water and set aside.

Pound the peanuts in a mortar or whizz in a food processor until finely ground.

Pound, grind or blend the drained chillies, shallots, garlic, candlenuts or macadamia nuts and lemongrass together to make a paste.

Heat the oil in a wok or heavy-bottomed saucepan and fry the chilli paste for 3 minutes. Add the coconut milk and bring to the boil, stirring constantly. Add the tamarind water, ground peanuts, sugar and salt to taste and cook for 5 minutes. If too thick, thin with up to 250 ml/8 fl oz water.

# Nasi lemak (*Coconut rice*)

**SERVES 4–6**

275 g/10 oz long-grain rice
500 ml/16 fl oz coconut milk
½ teaspoon salt
1 pandan leaf, tied in a knot
  (optional)

Wash the rice under cold running water until the water runs clear. Drain well.

Put the coconut milk, salt and 250 ml/8 fl oz water in a saucepan and bring slowly to the boil, stirring constantly. Add the rice and pandan leaf, stir, then cover and leave over the lowest possible heat (use a heat-diffusing mat if necessary) for about 20 minutes, until the rice has absorbed all the liquid and small holes have formed in the top. Remove from the heat and fluff up with a fork. Cover and leave in a warm place for up to 20 minutes.

# Classic Cooking

STARTERS

**Jean Christophe Novelli** Chef/patron of Maison Novelli, which opened in London to great acclaim in 1996. He previously worked at the Four Seasons restaurant, London.

VEGETABLE SOUPS

**Elisabeth Luard** Cookery writer for the *Sunday Telegraph Magazine* and author of *European Peasant Food* and *European Festival Food*, which won a Glenfiddich Award.

GOURMET SALADS

**Sonia Stevenson** The first woman chef in the UK to be awarded a Michelin star, at the Horn of Plenty in Devon. Author of *The Magic of Saucery* and *Fresh Ways with Fish*.

FISH AND SHELLFISH

**Gordon Ramsay** Chef/proprietor of one of London's most popular restaurants, Aubergine, recently awarded its second Michelin star. He is the author of *A Passion for Flavour*.

CHICKEN, DUCK AND GAME

**Nick Nairn** Chef/patron of Braeval restaurant near Aberfoyle in Scotland, whose BBC-TV series *Wild Harvest* was last summer's most successful cookery series, accompanied by a book.

LIVERS, SWEETBREADS AND KIDNEYS

**Simon Hopkinson** Former chef/patron at London's Bibendum restaurant, columnist and author of *Roast Chicken and Other Stories* and the forthcoming *The Prawn Cocktail Years*.

VEGETARIAN

**Rosamond Richardson** Author of several vegetarian titles, including *The Great Green Gourmet* and *Food from Green Places*. She has also appeared on television.

PASTA

**Joy Davies** One of the creators of *BBC Good Food Magazine*, she has been food editor of *She, Woman* and *Options* and written for the *Guardian, Daily Telegraph* and *Harpers & Queen*.

CHEESE DISHES

**Rose Elliot** The UK's most successful vegetarian cookery writer and author of many books, including *Not Just a Load of Old Lentils* and *The Classic Vegetarian Cookbook*.

POTATO DISHES

**Patrick McDonald** Author of the forthcoming *Simply Good Food* and Harvey Nichols' food consultant.

BISTRO COOKING

**Anne Willan** Founder and director of La Varenne Cookery School in Burgundy and West Virginia. Author of many books and a specialist in French cuisine.

ITALIAN COOKING

**Anna Del Conte** is the author of *The Classic Food of Northern Italy* (chosen as the 1996 Guild of Food Writers Book of the Year) and *The Gastronomy of Italy*. She has appeared on BBC-TV's *Masterchef*.

## Vietnamese Cooking

**Nicole Routhier** One of the United States' most popular cookery writers, her books include *Cooking Under Wraps*, *Nicole Routhier's Fruit Cookbook* and the award-winning *The Foods of Vietnam*.

## Malaysian Cooking

**Jill Dupleix** One of Australia's best known cookery writers, with columns in the *Sydney Morning Herald* and *Elle*. Author of *New Food*, *Allegro al dente* and the Master Chefs *Pacific*.

## Peking Cuisine

**Helen Chen** Learned to cook traditional Peking dishes from her mother, Joyce Chen, the grande dame of Chinese cooking in the United States. The author of *Chinese Home Cooking*.

## Stir fries

**Kay Fairfax** Author of several books, including *100 Great Stir-fries*, *Homemade* and *The Australian Christmas Book*.

## Noodles

**Terry Durack** Australia's most widely read restaurant critic and co-editor of the *Sydney Morning Herald Good Food Guide*. He is the author of *YUM!*, a book of stories and recipes.

## North Indian Curries

**Pat Chapman** Started the Curry Club in 1982. Appears regularly on television and radio and is the author of eighteen books, the latest being *The Thai Restaurant Cookbook*.

## Barbecues and Grills

**Brian Turner** Chef/patron of Turner's in Knightsbridge and one of Britain's most popular food broadcasters; he appears frequently on *Ready Steady Cook*, *Food and Drink* and many other television programmes.

## Summer and Winter Casseroles

**Anton Edelmann** Maître Chef des Cuisines at the Savoy Hotel, London, and author of six books. He appears regularly on BBC-TV's *Masterchef*.

## Traditional Puddings

**Tessa Bramley** Chef/patron of the acclaimed Old Vicarage restaurant in Ridgeway, Derbyshire. Author of *The Instinctive Cook*, and a regular presenter on a new Channel 4 daytime series *Here's One I Made Earlier*.

## Decorated Cakes

**Jane Asher** Author of several cookery books and a novel. She has also appeared in her own television series, *Jane Asher's Christmas* (1995).

## Favourite Cakes

**Mary Berry** One of Britain's leading cookery writers, her numerous books include *Mary Berry's Ultimate Cake Book*. She has made many television and radio appearances and is a regular contributor to cookery magazines.

First published in 1997 by
George Weidenfeld & Nicolson
The Orion Publishing Group
Orion House
5 Upper St Martin's Lane
London WC2H 9EA

British Library Cataloguing-in-Publication data
A catalogue record for this book is available from
the British Library

ISBN 0 297 82279 9

Designed by Lucy Holmes
Edited by Maggie Ramsay
Food styling by Joy Davies
Typeset by Tiger Typeset